From Uniform to Uniform

Transitioning from the Military to the Civilian Job Market

RICHARD L. AGEE

ISBN-10: 1500395625

ISBN-13: 978-1500395629

DEDICATION

Dedicated to the men, women, and their families who sacrificed more than most Americans will ever realize to provide the freedoms we so often take for granted. My hope for you, as you move into your next adventure in life, is that the nation's business world will provide as supporting and rewarding a career for you as you have for our nation.

CONTENTS

ACKNOWLEDGMENTS

Creation of a book always takes more than I think it does when I sit down to face a blank screen and computer keys to start writing. The material in this book comes from a lifetime of listening to soldiers and family members as they search for and attain jobs. It comes from human relations friends like Irene Harrington, Sally Daniel, and Donna McIlveen who helped me with my transition from military retirement to the corporate world. And I must thank my wife, Carole who faithful puts up with me when I become absent from the family, at least mentally when I get engrossed in a section or chapter that bugs me or intrigues me or I just can't seem to let go of until she hits me over the head with something.

PROLOGUE

Congratulations on your transition from one uniform to another. You'll find there is life after the service. Make your next career one you thoroughly enjoy. Take the time to figure out what you want in life and go for it. Find your purpose and fulfill it every day. Work will no longer be a burden, but a joy. When you fulfill your purpose, you find more than adequate compensation through the good you do for others.

Thank you for your past service. More service lies before you as you work in a career you truly love. It will provide meaningful work for you and needed help for others. It might even be profitable and fun.

1 WHAT DO I DO NOW?

What is it about military folk that cause us to think we are invincible? Perhaps it's the slogans we hear from the time recruiters begin to call us.

"We do more before nine o'clock than most people do all day."

"Be part of the action." "We're looking for a few good men." "An Army of one." "It's not a job, it's an adventure."

Maybe it's the training military members take and the values instilled in them through that training. They learn the importance of the individual as a member of the team and will sacrifice all for the good of the team and accomplishment of the mission.

Maybe it's the fact that the average age of our military force is so young. At eighteen and twenty, I never thought about death or dying. That's what old people did. If I took a round in battle, the medics would fix me. I could stare death in the face without fear. Death was a long way off despite the dangers posed by the job at hand.

For whatever reason, the thoughts of invincibility embedded in our young force carry across our military members throughout their career. It creates good leaders on the battlefield. It causes the scenes witnessed at disasters, where crowds run from the point of danger ... except for the handful of military, police, and firefighters who run toward the crisis.

This sense of invincibility creates a problem for our men and women leaving the service, however. Our newly discharged veterans assume their prowess on the battlefield will make them equally able to fight and win the battle for job placement in the commercial world they will soon enter. The delusion puts our veterans at incredible risk in our society with an unemployment rate 10% higher than the rest of society at the time of this writing and an underemployment rate reaching almost 50%. Another staggering statistic in the headlines about new veterans in the commercial job market reads, "New Vets Retain First Job Less than Six Months."

Eventually, everyone leaves the service. Some retire, some receive medical discharges, some receive discharges for one reason or another, some decide not to re-enlist, but everyone leave the service one way or another.

Congress finally discovered most are not prepared for the separation and instituted the Veterans Opportunity to Work Act (VOW) in 2011 to give assistance to new veterans. In the current economy, the Act is falling short. Perhaps partly, but not fully because of failures or shortfalls of the Act, but because veterans are not taking advantage of the Act and using it to fully prepare themselves for what's ahead.

Preparation wins the battle

Before a battle, commanders analyze every detail of plans. They know the enemy, the terrain, their own capabilities. they examine every aspect of the battle ahead and write and rewrite the battle plans until they mitigate every risk they can. Risk still remains. Unknowns linger. The battle isn't won yet. But everything they can know, they know. Only then will a commander put troops in harms way. Those troops went through months of individual and collective training as well. They know each other and their capabilities and weaknesses.

The Army recently announced it will reduce the force by 180,000 members. Meet John, a 14-year veteran with a wife and two kids, one with special needs. His specialty and rank is one targeted as significantly over-strength and within the next year, John will receive notice he will be part of the Reduction in Force (RIF). What will he do? He has a wife and two kids. What does a tanker have to offer the world?

John faces the reality of today. The security once resident in military service disappeared a few years ago and the promises of benefits, the GI Bill, VA benefits, so many perks that were part of the veteran's benefits on release from duty are no longer available due to lack of funding through decades of over- spending in our federal system.

Congress attempts to update programs, but trying to fix programs designed in the aftermath of World War II into today's society is like replacing the wings of a plane while in flight. The VOW Act is just one example. It attempts to help, but the execution is underfunded and poorly executed in most places. Consequently, the veteran's best source of help is not the assistance programs founded by the VOW Act, but in the veteran's own research, personal training, and preparation for the next phase of life.

Veteran unemployment and underemployment stands at 10-20% above the national average in most cities. 50-70% of the homeless population are veterans across the nation. As service men and women move from station to station, spouses with careers must begin again as well. Seldom do moving spouses receive appropriate credit for years worked or experience gained. They start at the bottom with every new job and are stymied in their career progression as they move with their military spouse from station to station. Consequently, the service member's separation from the service affects both the veteran and their spouse in a depressed economy.

Additionally, the media, in its attempt to aid veterans with its focus on post traumatic stress (PTS) and traumatic brain injuries (TBI) occurring in record numbers in the present day conflicts inadvertently characterized the majority of service members as damaged by their service. The most significant debilitations become the highlight of news casts and like most news stories, the focus exaggerates reality to the detriment of the majority of service members transitioning without issues.

The reality is that as of this writing in 2014, fewer than 45% of all service members have deployed into combat zones and fewer than 30% of those deployed have any form of PTS or TBI. If you do the math, that's less than 14% of the force with any problem and very few of those demonstrate any degree of debilitation. Still, the veteran faces the prejudice set up by the media when applying for a job.

Values

The Army uses the acronym LDRSHIP to help soldiers remember the values of the institution. Those values are:

- Loyalty

- Duty

- Respect

- Selfless Service

- Honor

- Integrity

The importance of values cannot be understated when operating under the stress of combat. They hold teams together in battle in the face of overwhelming odds. The Army values are not just words to soldiers. Soldiers live them and over time become part of the fiber of a soldier's very being. For commercial employers these can be good. But the veteran must learn new rules when engaging with the commercial world.

Loyalty

Loyalty in particular comes to mind. In fact, loyalty to troops changes only with the changing of laws enacted by Congress. But in the commercial world, loyalty often comes tied to the bottom line. As long as you earn your keep, you stay. As soon as you stop earning your keep, you're gone. Loyalty lasts exactly that long. If you've been with the company five days or fifty years, the same rule applies. Pay for yourself or hit the street.

John, and others like him, often take the first job available to get cash in their pocket whether it's the right job or not. Then within a few months, are fired because they weren't the right fit. As soon as John or his fellow soldiers saw the job wasn't what they thought from the description, they knew it wouldn't work, but stick around in the wrong job because they said they'd take the job and feel loyal to the company. The company doesn't feel the same loyalty. The company tries to make it work for a few months because of the cost of hiring, but firing comes pretty quickly.

2 WHAT DO I WANT TO DO?

John heard the stories from some of his buddies about the economy, the job market, the transition process. He's worried. What will he and his family do if he gets a pink slip from the Army? He knew he needed to start thinking early about what happens next in his life. But what could he do with 14 years in the Armor Corps? How does that relate to the civilian world?

For John and many of his contemporaries thinking through what's next is not an easy assignment. He trained from the day he entered the Army to "engage and destroy America's enemies." How do you turn that into a competitive resume? How do you make that sound appealing to the commercial world against the plethora of college graduates coming out with internships, multiple degrees, and career-assisted headhunting?

The first problem for John, is figuring out who he is apart from the Army. His identity equated to his rank and skill set within a structured military hierarchy for so long, he doesn't know how to think outside that structure. John is much more than SSG Romano, Assistant Platoon Sergeant and 1st Squad Leader for his platoon. But how does he describe that to an unknowing human relations specialist?

John didn't ask to be a squad leader. He didn't ask to be a staff sergeant. He didn't even ask to be part of the Armor Corps. When he joined, he asked to be a medic. Unfortunately, his math skills were a shade too low to make the cut and the Army needed tank drivers at the time. The recruiter told him what he would train for. After all the training, he found the work satisfying and he could get promoted faster than his medic friends, so armor wasn't so bad. But what now? If his number comes up for separation from the military, what does he really want to do with the rest of his life?

As a child John dreamed of fighting fires and driving ladder trucks. He played with hoses and used his imagination to douse the most horrific conflagrations. Then he'd go back to the fire station and cook gourmet meals for his buddies before turning in for the night and getting ready for the next alarm. John also thought about becoming a pilot and small band leader. He dreamed of being a car repair shop owner and the inventor of something that would revolutionize the world.

What does that have to do with today? It's time to look at a second career. Nearly 75% of Americans do not like their job and would leave it if they felt secure in doing so. John has an opportunity to make a clean start. Why not do something he likes instead of settling for just a job? If we have an opportunity to enjoy our work instead of just working, why not go for it? Why not take advantage of our skills, talents, experiences, and desires, put them all together and find the position that will let us capitalize on them? Why not enjoy life instead of feeling stuck with what we have?

The problem with most people, veterans and non-veterans alike, is that we accept the choice someone else makes for us as the path we must follow. The Army told John he would be in armor and so he was. Of course, John always had the choice of not re- enlisting, but he chose to continue his career in the armor instead.

Desires

So where does John start?

Start with daydreams. If money were no object and you could do anything in the world for the rest of your life, what would it be? What makes your eyes light up when you talk about it? What do you do that your friends slap you across the head to finally make you quit talking about it?

What are you madly passionate about?

For homework, write down a detailed description of your perfect job. Just one caveat. Your perfect job should not be your hobby. When you turn your hobby into your job, you no longer have a hobby to turn to for stress relief and relaxation. With that one exception, the sky is the limit. Make your dream job as descriptive and vivid as possible. Make it the thing you could do forever if you only had the time and money to do it right now. The thing you'd give anything to do.

Describe your perfect job with all the color and detail you can right now.

Skills and talents

Step two in the process of redefining yourself and finding that perfect second career is figuring out your skills and talents. Often, people limit themselves to the skill sets inherent in the job description of past jobs, regurgitating the activities and skills learned in the jobs they've done in the past or the knowledge they've gained through their educational pursuits.

Your skills and talents might far exceed those in your job description. Use the following thoughts to help stimulate what you really know and do, that match your desires for your next career.

Thinking of your past job descriptions, what specific skills did you use to accomplish those activities you listed?

In other areas of your life, such as church, school, clubs, home, what skills have you used in which others comment that you excel.

Look beyond the obvious in your activities to find secondary skills necessary for task accomplishment such as leadership, organization, particular technical knowledge such as the use of Office products, or other specific computer software.

What knowledge or expertise do you have as a result of your years in a particular field whether from work, study, or outside activities?

It's important to know your strengths and

weaknesses before you begin to think about your next career. Too often people jump into a career field they think they might be interested in without thinking about the skills required. If the requirements for the job include your weaknesses, think very hard before looking into that area any farther. The reason is because although we can improve our weak areas, they will seldom get better than mediocre. You'll be competing against others with expert skills in that area, so you will struggle continuously striving to improve and always watching people handle the tasks easily because it is their strength and not yours.

Look at careers that match your strengths. Don't waste time trying to improve weaknesses, instead become expert in your strengths. Think of those things you do without trying. Things you take for granted that you think everyone must know how to do. Trust me, they don't. Those are the areas of your strength. Improve those. Become expert in them until no one can compete with you in those areas. You'll find you are never without work when you find your unique skills.

So now, make an inventory of your skills, talents,

and abilities.

RICHARD AGEE

Experiences

Many veterans begin thinking of experience and express it in the same way on resumes and job interviews.

"I was a gunner in an infantry squad." "I was a platoon leader in a Cavalry company." "I was a battalion commander."

The human relations specialist across the table or reading the resume stares blindly at the page with no understanding of what those terms mean or how they equate to anything in the commercial market. Remember that as of 2013, less than 1% of the American population served in the military. Your chances of the sweet young lady reading your resume understanding your skills sets as a sergeant or captain are nil.

So what do you do?

Begin listing your experiences. What did you really do in those positions? As a gunner you did a lot more than shoot bullets. How did your job relate to the positions you might be interested in? Did you determine supply requirements? Did you perform maintenance? Did you conduct and lead training? Were you responsible for others in a supervisory role? Think of the attributes that go along with the position you held, not just the fact that you were a gunner or platoon leader or battalion commander. Those are "so what" titles on a resume. Describe the "so what" to yourself.

The next step in describing your experiences captures accomplishments. These cannot be fluffy, walk on water accolades that generally appear in efficiency reports. Think through your career and remember those accomplishments you look back on with pride and say, "I did that!" Approach them with this formula:

Problem + Action = Results

What problem did you see that you could fix, or what problem were you given to fix? It's always better if you saw the problem, but either way works. What did you do it fix the problem? What was the outcome?

State the outcome in terms of dollars saved or earned whenever possible.

Sometimes it's hard to think in terms of dollars in the federal sector because our budget systems are so different than the commercial world. The federal government doesn't think in terms of profit and loss. However, when you save time, it equates to man-hours and man-hours equate to money. When you reduce risk, you save potential lost days due to injury and that again equals potential man-days and money. If you save supplies or equipment, or extend the life of equipment, it equals money. Everything we do eventually comes back to the cost of doing business, even in the federal government. Anytime you think of accomplishments, work hard to put it back in terms of dollars saved through manpower, productivity, lower risk, or similar terms, so those reading the accomplishments will understand in their terms what you really did. Remember, these accomplishments are not for your reading pleasure, they are meant for the non-military world you are entering.

Complete the chart on the next page, filling in your top five to ten accomplishments in terms of Problem, Action, Results.

Once you complete the exercise of writing out your top five to ten accomplishments, prioritize them.

Position/ Date	Problem	Action Taken	Outome

Do not go back further than ten years unless you have something that is really remarkable. Winning the Nobel Prize, Medal of Honor, Silver Star, etc. Employers are interested in what you can do now, not ancient history, so ten years is about the outer limit for accomplishments. Put your accomplishments in order of importance to you first, but prepare to put them in the order of what might be important to your potential employer. Read through his eyes. All the while, think in terms of

Problem + Action = Results.

Purpose

Stepping into the spiritual component we all have and nurture in one way or another, all of us, with our unique set of desires, skills, talents, and experiences have a unique purpose in life. That purpose is not necessarily defined by our job or career, although we can express it through our career. But rather, our purpose in life is better expressed in our interaction with others in all our activities - job, home, neighborhood, church...

The problem most of us contend with throughout most of our life is that we never try to figure out our purpose. Instead we let others choose our path for us and we struggle through life doing what someone else thought we should do instead of what we are uniquely suited or created to do. A good friend, Clarence Lowe, puts it this way:

> *"I can sit on a table, but it doesn't work very well as a chair because it wasn't created to be a chair. It works fine as a table, because its purpose is to be a table. It's a terrible chair because it was not created for that purpose. We are each created with a specific purpose in mind."*

When you joined the military, the recruiter probably gave you one or two choices for your future specialty. The choices probably had little to do with your long term desires, but rather with the needs of the service. If they needed truck drivers, that was the specialty they pushed because that was the need. If they needed medics, they screened everyone for that potential to fill the ranks. Recruitment had far less to do with what you wanted than what the services needed at the time.

Over time, you probably came to learn the skill well and maybe progressed rapidly because of your aptitude for the skills that specialty required. However, because you have skills in one area, doesn't mean you're happy doing that job. As you look toward your next career, especially if retiring from the service, your career should be something you truly enjoy. Too many people already dislike their jobs, you do not want to add to the pool of dissatisfied employees.

Finding your purpose in life will help move you into a career field you truly love. So how do you go about discovering your purpose?

Start with your obituary. Perhaps that sounds a little crazy and morbid at first, but think about what you want people to say about you when you're gone. What kind of legacy do you want to leave? How do you want your children, grandchildren, and friends to remember you? Don't just think about it, write it down. Take some time and identify the things that you want to leave your family and the world. Your legacy will probably have nothing to do with houses, businesses, money, or other material things. It will deal with your character, your values, your moral compass in life.

How I want others to remember me:

Once you complete your obituary, set it aside and think through your values. What are the things that are important enough that you would spend the rest of your life in prison rather than compromise them. These will be things like family, integrity, your faith, and a few others. Expect the list to stay pretty short. There are not many things that will create such deep visceral reactions. Those are your values. Make a list. Write them down.

My values:

Think about your perfect job. What would you want to do for the next 300 years if money were no consideration. Think of some of the things you have done in the past that made your eyes light up. Those things that made you feel like a kid on Christmas morning. Hard to sleep the night before in anticipation of the event you will take part in tomorrow. The things that when people ask about them, they finally have to tell you to stop talking because you are so excited about the project or event. Things in which you lose all track of time and just pour yourself into them without thought of anything else. You described your perfect job in Chapter 2, describe it again now that you've looked at your skills, desires, legacy, and values.

Describe that perfect job in detail. Write it down. My Perfect Job:

Enhance your earlier perfect job description with more detail.

RICHARD AGEE

Next take the lists of your skills, talents, and experiences along with your obituary, values, and perfect job and lay them side-by-side to begin to get a picture of who you are. Think about the following as you discover your purpose:

The value you provide to people. What do you do to help them?

The activities you perform. How you help?

The resources you have. Skills, talents, and experiences.

The people you help. Individuals or demographic groups.

The weaknesses you have where you need others to support you in your mission and purpose.

All the information you gather to this point will help you discover your unique purpose in life. It will involve something bigger than you and will involve others. We are relational people and need each other. Someone needs what you do in fulfilling your purpose, just as you need others. No one makes it through life alone.

With all the work you've done to this point, complete the following sentences:

"My purpose in life is:

"I fulfill my purpose by:

When you can finish these two sentences that have little to do with any particular job or career, you will be on your way to finding fulfillment in whatever you do. From the evaluation of these two sentences, you can work out the job opportunities that will move you toward fulfilling your purpose, and you can narrow your focus on the things that you were created to do.

3 THIS IS JUST THE BEGINNING

What do you do with all the things you collected to discover your purpose and all the skills, talents, experiences, and desires that brought you to this point? Too many people leaving their former career assume this is the end of their effort in finding a new career. Now it's just a matter of finding the workplace that fits your purpose and everything will fall in place. Just throw out your contact information and let people know that you are available and the world will fall at your feet trying to give you a job.

When the unemployment rate falls below 2%, job

hunting might work that way. At that point, there are more jobs than people to fill them. Corporations scramble to fill their ranks with qualified candidates. The opposite is true with today's economy and unemployment topping 7%. Corporations have more candidates for jobs than they have jobs.

Congress enacted several laws over the last few years to try to help veterans in securing jobs, but the bottom line for corporations remains the same - the bottom line. Although many companies pledge to give positions to veterans today, many veterans are not prepared for the transition and stay in the job less than six months. The cost of bringing on another employee and training them for the job is not cheap.

Current averages show that it costs half of the employee's salary to on-board a new person and get them ready for the position they fill. And remember, that average cost is for all candidates, veteran or non- veteran, screened for skills, talents, education, and experience.

This in part explains why unemployment and underemployment among recently transitioned veterans is higher than their civilian counterparts. If the average veteran stays in their first job after transition for less than six months, the company never recoups their recruitment costs.

You would never go into battle without rigorous training to prepare you for the battlefield and the situations you are likely to encounter. Yet few service members think about the training they should do prior to transition to prepare them for the significant change they will experience on leaving the service. Many assume jobs will be easy to find because they have five or ten or twenty years of service. Remember the company's bottom line!

Companies love to hire veterans - that are qualified for the position! But they cannot afford to hire unqualified veterans or veterans that cannot be trained within a short period of time. Therefore, it's imperative that as a future veteran, you begin early to prepare for transition. Find out the skills you're lacking. Figure out courses you should complete before you leave the service. You'll never have more time than now to complete those things. Get started. The next several months will entail a lot of hard work getting ready for your next career.

4 WHERE TO LOOK FOR THE PERFECT JOB

Now you know your purpose in life. You know your skills, talents, experiences, and desires. You have a good idea of what you'd like to do. You've thought about what you would do if money didn't matter. You know, if money weren't an issue, what you would do for the next 300 years if possible. The question is, how do you find that position. Where do you start looking for that perfect job?

Begin with the Internet. Plug in your perfect job and see what comes up. You'll probably be surprised at the number of entries about people or companies doing exactly what you'd like to do. Few things are new in the world and probably your perfect job isn't new either. Take a look and see what others are doing and where you might find your perfect job.

Online job search tools like Monster.com, CareerBuilder.com, FindtheRightJob.com, JobsResource.com and many others are available to assist you in your search. Be aware, however, that for every job listed on the Internet, you'll compete with dozens if not hundreds of others for the position through online applications. This doesn't mean you should ignore these sites or fail to submit applications, but a reminder that competition is keen and your resume must sparkle.

Another way to find your perfect job is through talking with like-minded people. In your Internet search, find the CEO, COO, or manager within the company or agency which mirrors your perfect job. Read recent news reports about the company or individual. If the person you find has written a book, an article, or an interview, find it and read it.

Once you collect information about the manager in reference to your perfect job, make an appointment with him. Your appointment is not about getting hired, but about how you can attain what you want to do. Remember, this person is doing or is leading exactly what you determined is the perfect job for you. You're passionate about it. You love the idea of what is happening in his company and in his work life. You want to learn from him how you can get to the place he has arrived.

With that attitude and perspective in mind, your appointment is a mentoring experience, not a job interview. Make sure you come prepared with meaningful questions based on what you've learned so far. Find out the manager's story.

What brought him to this place?

What unique qualifications do you need to move into that perfect job?

What education, certification, or licensing requirements must you meet?

What kinds of experience allow you to advance to the job you're looking for?

You are there to find out from someone who has been there what you need to do to get into the same business. Never lose sight of that objective in your meeting.

Dress as you would for a job interview. Be on time and leave on time. Prepare yourself well before you meet with the mentor you chose. Take a copy of your resume geared to apply for your perfect job with you. (We'll talk more about your resume in the next chapter.)

Often one of two things happen in mentor relationships as I've described above. One, the mentor recognizes your enthusiasm, drive, skills, and experience and hires you.

Two, the mentor knows someone else looking for a recruit with your skills and talents and will refer you to them. An interesting bit of information the Department of Labor doesn't tell you is that 70% of all jobs are created for a person. They are not filled through online applications. This hiring practice is particularly true for mid to senior management positions.

Why do managers use this practice? Two reasons. First, they see your talent and passion concerning your perfect job and know you will make money for them.

Second, they fear their competitors will hire you and take away some of their business. In either case, when managers meet someone so passionate about a career as to do what you just did, they see it as an economic advantage to their business to bring you on board.

The secret to success with this approach, is to make your interview based on the manager's mentorship, not on your request for a job. Don't even let the mentor know you have a resume with you until you stand up to leave. Have good questions and take good notes.

Whether you end up with an interview for a position or not, you will learn more about what to do and how to secure your perfect job.

When your appointment is at its close, thank the mentor for the information and leave a copy of your resume. Let him know that if he knows anyone looking for someone with your skills and experience, you would appreciate his help and referral. Leave before he has time to read your resume. If he liked you and has a position or can create a position, he'll call you back.

Use the same approach for all of the companies and positions you found interest in during your initial search. Yes, it takes time and work to approach jobs this way, but you will likely find this approach much more successful than sitting at home filling out applications.

5 SELLING YOURSELF

Selling yourself includes four principle areas you'll need to pay particular attention to in order to prepare for your next career:

- your resume

- your appearance or look

- your language

- your interview

We'll look at each of these in order and determine how to approach each and what you can do to make yourself more presentable to prospective employers.

The Resume

The resume usually represents the first step in getting past human relations (HR) departments. We talked about ways to get through HR and gatekeepers in the last chapter, "Where to Look." Still, the resume plays an important role in giving perspective employers a glimpse of who you are and what you can do.

For that reason, write resumes in response to the specific job for which you apply. If you try to use a general, one-size-fits-all resume for every position on your list, you are likely to find yourself at the bottom of the stack with no interviews and no job.

So what should a resume include and how do you write one that will give a good and honest appraisal of who you are and what you can bring to the company? Those are the two things to keep in mind as you prepare any resume.

What can you do and what value do you bring to the company to which you apply?

A good resume will include the following parts:

- Heading/contact information
- Summary

- Accomplishments

- Experience

- Education/certifications/license

Heading/contact information

A few things to remember in the heading. Include your name, address, phone number, and email address. Your address should be your mailing address so contacts can send information, on-boarding packets, and so forth.

Make sure the phone number is one that will always be answered. Having an inexpensive answering machine or voice mail is well worth the investment rather than a HR representative getting no answer. Then be sure to check voice mail or your answering machine at least twice a day near noon and close of business.

HR representatives and executive assistants often make calls near those times after they have spent the morning or afternoon researching and filtering potential candidates.

Finally, keep your email address something that looks and sounds professional. Using hotmail, yahoo, AOL, or other mail service is fine as long as your address sends the right message. Using an address like sweetiepie@... or warrior6@... or any other front end that portrays something other than professionalism needs revision.

Many services will let you open free email. Get one that reflects your professional side, like your name! Even if the only thing you ever use the email for is business, you'll find it well worth your effort to get an address without these cute titles.

Don't forget to check your email and your voice mail regularly. Jobs do not stay open long in today's economy. There may be anywhere from 10 to 100 qualified applicants vying for that position. You don't want to miss an opportunity for an interview because you failed to answer an email or listen to a voice mail. Or because the information on your resume was wrong or too cute for consideration. Think of your heading in terms of what the employer needs to find you - nothing more, but nothing less.

Summary

The summary section tells the reader what you want in your next job. It gives a short statement of your best skills and the personal goals you have in using those skills for your perspective employer.

The summary should be only a few lines and easy to read. Avoid industry jargon, clichés, and fluff. Tell the reader your top skills and goals, then quit.

Accomplishments

The accomplishments section is the most important part of the resume in my opinion. The four or five paragraphs that make up this part of your resume tell the reader what you can bring to the company because of your past accomplishments. Sounds simple, but too many people use this section to give a laundry list of job descriptions of past assignments instead of focusing on their accomplishments.

Go back to the chart you completed earlier in which you described your accomplishments in terms of problem, actions, and results (PAR). The PAR formula will better serve you as others try to determine your true capabilities and value to the perspective firm.

As you review your results, write them in terms of what the reader wants to hear. A for-profit business needs to know you will make three times more for the company than your salary. If they don't see the return on investment in terms of bottom line for the company, don't expect to make it into an interview.

Non-profit and government agencies want to see value added as well, but may not be as hard on the bottom line figures. They still need to see accomplishments. How can you help them save time, money, or effort in their projects? Show your perspective employer you add value to their firm or agency by picking past accomplishments relating to what they do as an organization or company.

Once you've developed your list of accomplishments, put the top four or five into your resume. Make sure the accomplishments can be verified if the employer choses to do so and state them honestly and clearly. If you were the leader of the team, take credit for what the team did, but ensure you address the leadership part if you did not participate in the hands-on technical issues. Don't write things that might be construed as dishonest when your perspective employer calls a reference about what you've said in your resume.

Experience

Experience is where you give your laundry list of assignments. In reverse chronological order, give your position title in non-military and non-jargon words. Few outside the military understand the role, responsibility, or job description of a platoon leader. Translate your position title into something those who will read it understand.

Give the name of the company or organization and the dates you filled the position. Go back not more than ten years and summarize any earlier positions unless they are absolutely germane to the position for which you apply. Anything older than ten years is ancient history in today's business environment due to the changes in the economy, industry, and technology. Concentrate on those positions that will win the job.

Education/certification/license

The next section of your resume lays out your formal education. Whether you list education in chronological or reverse chronological order is up to you. It often helps to have the highest degree listed first, however, to save readers time. If they see you have the requisite education or certification, seldom will they read the rest of the section until you are in the final throws of selection.

Certifications and license are critical if your specialty requires them. Certifications and license show you are active in the field. Most employers prefer certifications and license to degrees because you usually must be actively working in the field to obtain and maintain these qualifications.

If you don't have a needed certification or license, start working on it and state when you expect to have the certification or license in your hand. Let your perspective employer know you understand the need and you are actively working toward it. Make sure you get started because the employer may check the status with the organization to which you applied.

Other

You may add other sections to your resume in certain cases. For instance, if you hold a current security clearance, they are worth gold to federal contractors because it takes so long to get them today. If you are published, a list of books and articles you've authored is appropriate. If you were co-author, make sure you state so on the listed publications.

If you are a member of a board of directors for non-profit or for- profit firms, these show your interest in and commitment to the longevity of the community and might give you an edge on another candidate.

Some final thoughts about your resume.

One resume will not fit all job opportunities. In fact, one resume will not fill all job opportunities in the same industry and with the same title and job description. You need to do some homework and know exactly what a firm is asking. Find the keywords in their job announcement and make sure all of them appear in your resume.

Many recruiters use electronic search engines to make the first cut in potential candidates. You may be the best applicant, but if your resume doesn't include the keywords used in the initial screen, you will never get the interview. So, write a clean resume for each job for which you apply. The extra work will pay big dividends for you.

Second, if at all possible, keep your resume to not

more than two pages. The only thing that should appear on a third page are publications you've authored or items in the "other" category. Everything else should be visible on the first two pages. With hundreds of applicants for each new open position, few HR specialists read past the first page or page and a half of any resume. The fist page is always the most important and must have the keywords the recruiters look for.

Third, after you write your resume, set it aside for two or three days and then go back and rewrite it with fresh eyes. It also help to have someone else read it to see if they find errors in content, grammar, and spelling. One of the worst things you can do is submit a resume with misspelled words. Remember, too, your spell check may not catch the difference between there, their, and they're. All are spelled correctly, but their use in sentences is very different. Check your spelling! Then check your spelling! Finally, check your spelling! Don't let typos and careless errors get into the piece of paper that may mean the difference between employment and unemployment.

Finally, hand-carry a copy of your resume to firms

if they will accept it. There are several reasons for handing a copy to perspective employers. First, it shows you're interested enough to make the effort to come to the office. Second, it gives a first impression that can serve as a pre-interview session. Third, it is much harder for people to say "no" in person than through the Internet or over the phone. Give a copy of the resume to the highest person in the organization you can reach along with a copy to the HR department.

The Look

The workplace today is very different than 20 years ago when most business professionals wore suits and ties every day. Today, polo shirts, jeans, open collar shirts and slacks are the norm rather than the exception in many businesses. However, you are applying for a job and need to make a good first impression. So, how should you dress?

Applying in uniform is not appropriate. Just don't do it. You're entering the commercial market and need to look the part. The best way to figure out how to dress for an interview is to do some homework again. First, go to the Internet and look for every picture you can find of employees at the company to which you are applying. See what they wear every day in the workplace. Don't consider the Friday dress or company special event photos. Look for the pictures where they deal with customers during the week.

Next, drive by the business and watch people enter and leave the employee entrances. See what the dress is like for those coming and going into the building. Once you've done your homework, you know how casual or how business-like employees dress. Use that standard as the bottom line. If no one wears a tie, but some wear sport coats, the least you should wear is a sport coat for your interview. If most are in polo shirts and slacks, that becomes your minimum standard, but you're probably better off with a buttoned shirt. Use the average dress code as your *minimum standard* and think about dressing one step up. It never hurts to be overdressed in an interview, but dressing down can kill your first impression.

Under no circumstances should you wear a T-shirt or shorts. Remember you are trying to make a good impression on the HR department or interviewers. Neither should you wear a polo shirt with writing on it. Whether you think the slogan is good or bad doesn't matter. It's what the person interviewing thinks about it and you won't know until after you get to know them. The best advice is *never wear shirts with slogans* to an interview!

It shouldn't have to be said, but I've done too many interviews not to say it. Take a bath, use deodorant, brush your teeth, comb your hair, iron your clothes. Don't look like you crawled out of bed just in time to get there. It takes a few minutes of interview to hire someone, but you can be dismissed as a viable applicant in the first four seconds. It's a hard uphill climb if that happens. Be prepared visually.

The Language

Language is tough to change when you worked in the military or any job for several years with its peculiar jargon. We easily get into the habit of talking about leave instead of vacation, posts and stations instead of addresses, command instead of leadership and management. The commercial world knows little of the military. Remember, less than 1% of the population now has any affiliation with the military - no personal service, no siblings, parents, or extended family in the service. That means only a small percentage of people understand your jargon.

Even within the military our acronyms and jargon is misunderstood. For example, DFAS can mean Defense Finance & Accounting Service, Dark Field Alignment System, Defense Fuels Accounting System, or Division of Financial and Administrative Services. Add a couple of other DFAS acronyms like Decorative and Fine Arts Society and Department of Fisheries and Aquatic Sciences, and you begin to see how confusing language can get.

Begin now to get acronyms out of your language. Even if you are still on active duty, people will understand you better without acronyms. We develop and use acronyms because we think they save time. They don't. They just add to the confusion of communication and show others we are lazy in our speech. So get rid of acronyms as quickly as possible and begin using acceptable English as your form of communication.

Think about how best to translate your positions, roles, and responsibilities into language the commercial sector can understand. As mentioned earlier, platoon leader makes little sense to the commercial world. Battalion, squad, corps, company, wing, squadron, and all such descriptions mean little to the world outside the military. By converting your positions and leadership, responsibilities, and scale to intelligent commercial terms, you will go much further in the interview.

A company commander, for instance, is a mid-level manager with about a hundred employees. As commander, the scope of our responsibilities can exceed those of a mid-level manager in that you are solely accountable for training, supporting, and providing rewards and punishment for behavior and performance not normally given to managers in the commercial world.

At the same time, mid-level managers in the commercial market may have responsibility for profit and loss for their branch. Their failure means the loss of livelihood for the employees in their charge. If the division or section doesn't meet profit goals, workers get fired. Not so in the federal sector. The company commander doesn't have to worry about return on investments, profit and loss, production schedules, or marketing. Neither position is better or worse than the other, but the two draw similarities in terms of scope of responsibility.

Turning position titles and responsibilities into language the commercial side understands takes time and effort. The Transition Assistance Program provides services in this area, as does the Veterans' Administration, the Department of Labor, and other human relations organizations. Use them for their expertise before trying to draw conclusions yourself. That doesn't mean you must use their suggestions, but they will point you down the right path toward interpreting your resume for the commercial world.

The Interview

People usually abhor interviews. However, you can make them work to your benefit with the right preparation. You'll see individuals hyperventilating, sweating, making nervous gestures, and all sorts of other phenomena related to the stress they feel before going into the dreaded interview. This is what you worked for, though. This is the grand finale. Jobs are won or lost here. If you're not ready for the interview, everything you've done to get to this point has been wasted effort.

We've talked about how you look - clean, proper attire, neatly groomed. We've talked about language - getting rid of the acronyms and jargon. Now it's time to figure out what you take to the interview and how you approach it.

Unfortunately, there are not many good interviewers in the market. Not many of the HR specialists you'll meet in the corporations and companies you approach will have a good interview process. More often than not, the person on the other side of the desk from you will stare at your resume a few minutes, ask you a few questions about your resume and then ask some standard, yet meaningless questions.

• Why do you want to work with us?

• What did you do in your last job?

• Why did you leave your last job?

• What are your expectations in the next twelve months?

• How do you handle conflict?

• How much do you need to make in this position?

You want to take charge of the interview without the interviewer realizing it. Start by doing your homework on the company before you arrive. Get information from the Internet, library, Chamber of Commerce and any other source you can find to know as much about the company as possible. Study as if this test determines the direction of your career ... because it does! Know who the CEO is. Know as many of the senior executives as you can. Be familiar with the structure of the company and any recent awards or news items. Know how much revenue they make and where they stand in their industry.

Taking some time to learn about the company makes a huge difference in two things. It helps you know whether the company fits your purpose and values. With this information you know whether you should even be there. Second, your deep understanding of the company shows the HR specialist doing the interview that you want the job and know what you're stepping into.

Prepare your notebook for the interview. You'll

have at least two or three hard copies of your resume to give away. You'll have one copy marked with points you want to emphasize to the company. You'll have a copy of your personal budget, not for them, but for your review. You need to know what your bottom line must be to survive.

Have questions ready for the interviewer. In your research, you will discover things you want to ask for clarity. The interviewer usually tells you about company policies, vacation and sick time, benefits as they pertain to all employees, and so forth. Know what questions you want to ask to clarify any of those topics before you go.

Get a good night's sleep. Eat a light breakfast or if an afternoon interview, a light lunch. Don't gorge on food and find yourself sleepy in the interview. Eat enough to keep your energy level high, but not so much that you crash. Drink water before the interview to make sure you are hydrated. Think about all the things you would do before a physical fitness test to improve your score. Do those things. You'll find the physical and mental energy you exert in your interview will demand it.

Next, arrive early. Announce yourself to the receptionist or executive assistant and take the ten or fifteen minutes before your interview to watch the people in the office.

How do they interact with each other?

What is the tone of their conversations?

Look at the pictures and especially the certificates and awards on the office wall. Get a feel for the character of the office and its workers while you wait for your interview. If you've never done that before, you may find some of the actions a little shocking coming straight from a strict military hierarchy. Most people are on a first name basis regardless of whether they are file clerks or the vice president of the company. Seldom will you hear anyone say sir or ma'am. You will see some semblance of hierarchy, but usually more in the size and placement of the offices than anything else.

Take a few deep breaths, relax, think about your accomplishments from the list of ten you created earlier. You may want to use one or two of them other than those in your resume. You may also want to expand on the information in your accomplishments. Perhaps you review in your mind a more recent accomplishment that didn't get into your resume. You may think of more questions you want to ask the interviewer.

As you approach the interviewer, if you are female, extend your hand to make the first move to shake hands. If you are male, extend your hand to initiate a handshake if the interviewer is male. If the interviewer is female, let her extend her hand first. Shake hands with a firm, but not crushing grip. Look the interviewer in the eyes throughout the interview unless you are writing notes in your notebook. If there are more than one person interviewing, make eye contact with each and focus on the one you address answers and questions to. Unlike military briefings in which answers are given to the highest ranking individual or host of the briefing, you will address answers to the one who asked.

Sit up straight, but don't act like a West Point Cadet perched on the edge of the seat and ramrod straight. Relax and mirror your interviewers, but don't let yourself slouch if they do. Keep good posture. It will help your voice and your brain as blood flows more smoothly when you exercise good posture. Answer in a voice that is loud enough for everyone to hear without straining, but don't be overbearing. Leave your command voice at home.

One of the biggest complaints about veteran interviews is the perspective candidate appears too rigid and sounds like a drill sergeant. Remember most of your co-workers know nothing about the military except what they hear from the media and see in bad movies. None of which reflect accurately what military life is like or the persona of military members. Again, relax and talk to the interviewers like a friend.

Make sure your questions are answered. One of the misconceptions of job interviews is that the interviewee is on the hot seat to try and win a job. The other half of a job interview is seldom discussed. The other half is your interview of the company. Is this place the right fit for you? After seeing a few of the employees and going through the interview process, is this where you want to spend a third of your life for the next several years?

While in the military, you had little choice in

assignments. Now, you are fully in control of whether you accept a position offered. One of the reasons 70% of Americans are unhappy with their job is they fail to realize they also have control in the interview process. We do not have to accept a job that feels wrong.

Once you have answered all of the interviewer's questions and all of your questions are answered, don't prolong the interview. Everyone has other jobs to do and you want to leave, not chitchat. Thank the interviewer for his time and offer to leave a hard copy of your resume. Ask when you should hear from them and if there is anything else they need from you.

Don't expect to be offered a job at the interview. If you are, you have two choices. You can accept it (not a good idea to accept a job at an interview). Or you can thank them for the offer and ask, "When do I need to let you know my answer?" Think through the pros and cons of working for the company and get back to them with your answer before the deadline they gave you. A big part of your decision will probably involve finances and you need to make sure you don't make spur of the moment decisions about those things. We will cover more on finances in the next chapter.

6 NEGOTIATING FOR MONEY OR OTHER STUFF

Salary and benefits comprise two important parts of your job search. Even if you ace the interview and know it's the perfect job, you still need to make an income and survive in a rather unstable economy. How much are you worth to the company? How much do you need to have a comfortable standard of living?

Before you begin negotiations on salary and benefits, you MUST know your bottom line. If you've never created a budget before, now is the time to start. Before you approach a perspective employer with numbers, you need to know you will be able to live on what they pay you. If not, no matter how good the job may seem, you cannot take the job if you can't pay your bills. The job will soon become burdensome and you will not perform at your best. You will quit or be fired in short order and be left with resentment toward the company and maybe your career.

Know what you need to make. Take two or three months of your current obligations and know what you spend. What might be cut out or must be added when you move to the new position? Things transitioning veterans often forget are the things the military provided during your time in service. Things like healthcare insurance or supplements, rent or mortgage payments, utilities, cable, clothing (you'll probably need a new wardrobe), transportation costs, etc. Remember, several of the items you currently receive from the military in compensation are tax-free. They won't be in your commercial compensation. Remember to adjust for your taxes.

Once you know what you need, make a list of those recurring costs that might be tax-deductible for a business that you might leverage in benefits.

This is an important step. For everything the company supplies that you don't need to pay out of your pocket, you just received a pay raise.

For instance, if the company provides home Internet service so you can do some work from home, you just saved $30-40 per month in your personal expenses. If you do a great deal of local travel for the company and they will furnish a gas card for you, you just saved $300-400 a month in gas. If they require you to wear certain clothes in your job, uniforms or even a suit and will pay part or all of your laundry expense for those items, you've saved $100-200 a month in laundry bills. Look at everything you paid for over the last three months and see how much might be negotiated into benefits.

If retiring from the service, you will receive retirement pay that is taxable in most states. You will no doubt be in a new tax-bracket because of the extra income. Your retirement pay should not be a consideration in negotiating your salary unless you want it to be.

All of those items you might consider negotiating as benefits with your new boss, however, could significantly reduce your 'cash salary' and lower your total taxable income, thereby lowering your tax-rate. The balancing act you want to negotiate with your new employer is total compensation, not salary or benefits, but the total package.

These negotiations work much better with small businesses than large. Large businesses usually have set policies and guidelines for benefits in particular and will not make many exceptions for an individual employee. It is worth trying, however, because the worst they can tell you is no. If you don't ask, they don't have an opportunity to say yes.

Always think about benefits first because these normally remain tax-free and don't show up on your W-2 at the end of the year. The right benefits are like money in your pocket because they are expenses you don't have to bear. Work on the benefit package first! See how much you make with the benefit package before you begin talking about cash salary. Your salary makes up the difference between what your benefits pay for and what you'll need to pay the rest of your bills each month. Take a calculator with you to the salary negotiation.

Don't consider your retirement pay during salary negotiations. That's money you receive whether you work or not. If a perspective employer begins to talk about your military retirement pay, stop the conversation and get up to leave. Having said that, you can always consider it yourself if you want your perfect job and are willing to sacrifice some or all of your retirement pay to make ends meet with the salary you negotiate. Never think about it in terms of sacrificing salary and benefits. When you start to think you're sacrificing your retirement for your perfect job, you'll begin to dislike your job.

Let your perspective employer make the first move on how much he will pay you. If above what you needed, you can accept it as is or ask for a little more to see if he is willing to raise his salary for you. If he does, you're golden, if not, you still know you made more than you need. If the offer is less than you need, begin negotiations at a salary higher than your bottom line so that the real package you need is about half way between the two numbers. Remember, you are working with total compensation both from your need and your salary negotiations. Be sure you subtract the value of benefits the company provides in the negotiation as you consider the rest of your compensation.

Following this path, you'll find a satisfactory salary and benefits package you can be sure will meet your needs as you begin your new career.

7 CLOSING THOUGHTS

My prayer is that the exercises and thought processes you went through in these pages helped you focus on who you are and what you want in your next career. As mentioned earlier, the Army would never put you into battle without a great deal of training. Unfortunately, the same has not been true in preparing you to face your transition from one career to another.

You'll find the civilian market just as rewarding and almost as exciting as your military career, but in different ways. You can find your purpose in life and then fulfill it in a variety of ways. When you live your purpose, you can't help but find fulfillment and happiness.

For more help and insight, you can reach me at richard@ageesconsulting.com. I welcome your comments as well. I also invite you to visit my websites: wantalifecoach.com for information on balancing your life and finding purpose in life; and richardagee.com for a daily devotional called "Walk with Me."

I also invite you to read *The Dream*, my chronology of the development of the medical support plan for Operation Desert Storm, which changed medical concepts on the battlefield still in use today. You can purchase *The Dream* at amazon.com in paperback or in a Kindle edition.